Colin McNaughton
CRAZY BEAR

four crazy stories in one **big** book

Cowboy Crazy

Snow Crazy

Pirate Crazy

Rock and Roll Crazy

Holt, Rinehart and Winston
NEW YORK

Cowboy Crazy

It was Saturday morning. Bruno was at the movies watching a cowboy picture. It was great!

Here's a good guy.   There's a bad guy.   They're about to shoot

when suddenly – INDIANS!   Bruno was spellbound.

Was this the end for the Sheriff? No! By an amazing coincidence the chief was his long lost brother. Hooray!

"What a movie," thought Bruno as he left the theater. "I wish I'd been a cowboy."

He rushed home, dashed upstairs, and ransacked his toy cupboard. Five minutes later he came downstairs and there stood...

...Bruno the Kid!

Bruno decided to go into town. He leaped on his horse and rode off.

The place was deserted.

He left his horse on Main Street and went looking for trouble.

Suddenly, he heard a rumbling noise. BUFFALO! And they're coming this way. CLOSER...

...and CLOSER.

A whole herd of buffalo!

Bruno was outnumbered. He had to retreat.

When the coast was clear, he came out of his hiding place.

He looked around. Something caught his eye.

INDIANS!

He climbed the fence...

Once again Bruno the Kid had to flee, chased by hordes of furious Indians.

His horse was so powerful that he quickly left the enemy far behind. After days and days of hard riding across deserts and over mountains, he arrived back at the ranch.

But as he pushed open the backyard gate, he jumped back in horror! For there stood his worst enemy – BLACK JACK McDRAW.

They drew their guns at exactly the same moment and fired.

And they both bit the dust.

As Bruno was breathing his last breath, his mom came out.

"Come on, cowboy," she said. "Time to mosey on down to the chuck wagon; it's chow time."
And they went in for supper.

The End

Snow Crazy

2

"YAHOO! My favorite weather!" shouted Bruno when his mom woke him one morning with the news that it had been snowing all night.

He sprang out of bed, washed his face, quickly dressed, wolfed down his breakfast, put on his hat, snowsuit and scarf, pulled on his boots, brushed his teeth, and dashed outside.

"Don't slam the door," shouted his mom. But it was too late.

She ran out after him and said angrily,
"Bruno, I told you not to slam the door. There's snow on the... my goodness, that was quick, you've built a snowbear already!"

Suddenly the snowbear moved. It was Bruno. He shook off the snow and ran out to play.

None of his friends seemed to be around, so Bruno decided to go to the park.
"I'll roll the biggest snowball ever," he said to himself.
Unfortunately, he got carried away.
After that, everything just went downhill.

The huge snowball with Bruno inside it came to a halt. He was stunned.

But he soon recovered. Looking at the mound of snow, he had an idea.

He built an igloo!

With the igloo finished, he decided to go fishing — Eskimo-style.
"I'll fish in the fountain," thought Bruno.
He made a fishing rod from a twig and a piece of string.

But the fountain was iced over. He tried to break it. He almost slipped, which gave him another idea...

Bruno — Ice Skating Champion!

Then Bruno saw something. It looked like a fishing hole.

He was starting to get cold when suddenly...

. . . He caught a hat! A hat? Yes, a hat!

It was the hat of a workman in a manhole.

He wasn't very pleased.

Bruno was off! He ran all the way home and slammed the backyard gate.

"Ah, Bruno, there you are," said his mom. "Time to come in now."

"Aw, no, Mom," replied Bruno, "I want to stay out and play awhile longer."

"There's something on television you might like to watch," she said.

"Oh, what's that, Mom?" asked Bruno.

"*Snow White!*" said his mom.

"YAHOO!" cried Bruno. "My favorite movie."

And he went into the warm house.

The End

Pirate Crazy

3

It was Easter vacation, Bruno's parents had sent him to visit his rich Aunt Mimi.

Bruno liked his aunt. If only she wouldn't keep kissing him all the time! Bruno didn't like being kissed.

A taxi brought him from the railroad station to Aunt Mimi's lovely house in the country.

Aunt Mimi was so pleased to see Bruno that she kissed him. Then she gave him lots of money.

"Make sure you put it in a safe place," said his aunt. "Off you go and unpack, then you can play outside until suppertime."

In his bedroom Bruno was thinking to himself, "I wonder where I should put all this money? I know, I'll bury it. Buried treasure!"

Luckily, he had brought all his pirate clothes with him in his suitcase.

He was Bruno, the Swashbuckling Pirate.

Downstairs in the kitchen, he found an empty cookie box. "This will make a perfect treasure chest," said Bruno.

"But where can I bury my treasure?"

He wandered across the garden to some dense bushes.
"Let's see what's behind here," he said to himself as he cut a path with his sword.

And this is what he found!

An old dried-up fountain. "Oh, what a perfect place," thought Bruno.

He buried his treasure under a pile of rocks.

Back in his bedroom, Bruno drew a treasure map.

As he was finishing Aunt Mimi called to him, "Bruno, my angel, time for supper."

At the table she asked him what he'd been up to.

Bruno told her he'd found a wonderful place to hide his treasure. "But I can't tell you where," said Bruno. "It's a secret."

Bruno slept soundly that night. Outside, a terrible storm raged.

At breakfast the next morning, Aunt Mimi told him all about the storm and the rain.

"Oh, no!" cried Bruno, jumping up.

He ran out of the house and through the dripping jungle...

The fountain was full of water!

He sat down to think.

"I can't swim down because the water's too muddy," he said to himself. "What I really need is a boat. Then maybe I could sail out and knock the rocks off with a stick, then hook the treasure chest and pull it out. But where can I find a boat?"

He went back to the house and looked around. He found just what he was looking for. A rain barrel!

He tipped the water out and carried it back to the fountain.

Bruno launched the barrel.

It turned out to be more difficult than he imagined!

"This is hopeless," thought Bruno. "If only I could get all the water out...I know, I'll dig a trench into the side of the fountain. Easy as pie!"

He found a shovel in the toolshed...

...and started to dig. The sun was shining and it was hot. He sang a little song.

Meanwhile, down in the garden below Bruno, Aunt Mimi was sitting in the sun. Like Bruno, she was feeling rather warm. She heard Bruno singing behind her and called out, "Bruno, my darling, would you be an angel and get something to cool me off? Perhaps…"

> Bruno, what on earth have you been up to?

> Well, er, um, you did say you wanted something to cool you off.

The water came roaring through the garden like a tidal wave. It swept everything along in its path — including Bruno, the treasure, and Aunt Mimi.

"Bruno," spluttered Aunt Mimi when the flood was over, "what on earth have you been up to?"

"You did say you wanted something to cool you off," said Bruno, a little sheepishly.

"Oh Bruno!" cried Aunt Mimi, "What a rascal you are. But I forgive you. Let me kiss you!"

"Phew," sighed Bruno, and they went to get cleaned up.

The noise was deafening.

Bruno's rock and roll group, The Donuts, was rehearsing in his backyard.

Tomorrow was Saturday and they were playing at the local youth center. They had to get it right.

Halfway through their first song, "The Grizzly Bear Stomp", Bruno's mom popped her head out of the window and shouted: "BRUNO! BRUNO!"

"Yes, Mom?" said Bruno, when he finally heard her.

"You'll have to practice somewhere else, I'm afraid," she said. "I've got company, and we can't hear ourselves talk."

"OK, Mom," said Bruno. "Come on, you guys, we've got to move on."

"Where can we go?" asked Tex.

"My mom and dad are out shopping," said Roberto, "so we can practice in my bedroom."

But things were no better at Roberto's house.

They'd only been playing for a few minutes when Roberto's brothers and sisters started to complain that they couldn't hear the cartoons on television.

"Let's try the alley," said Patch.

As Bruno struck his guitar to start his first song, there was a howl of protest from behind the fence.

It was Leroy and his gang.

"Hey," shouted Leroy, "what's the big idea? We're trying to listen to the radio. Keep the noise down!"

"Come on," said Tex, "let's go over to the lake. Surely no one will mind us playing there."

The lake was just outside town; so off they went.

They piled into a rowboat and rowed out into the middle of the lake.

They had just started to sing "Bee bop a loo lop" when there were shouts of "Shut up! You'll frighten the fish!" from all around the banks of the lake.

"This is crazy!" said Bruno. "But let's try one last time. Hey, how about the top of the hill? There's never anyone up there."

They dragged, pushed, and pulled their equipment up the hill. Once again they struck up a tune.

Bee bop a loo lop...

"Bee bop a loo lop…" began Bruno.
There was a loud SSSHHH!
"HELP! SNAKES!" cried Patch.
But there were no snakes. Only birdwatchers.
"Stop that noise!" said one. "You'll scare the birds."
"I give up," said Bruno. "Come on, let's go home."
They struggled back to town and went their separate ways.

Bruno was worried. The concert was tomorrow night and they really hadn't rehearsed enough. But what could they do? Nothing. They just had to make the best of it.

It was Saturday night, the night of the dance. The Donuts were on stage setting up their instruments. Bruno was peering through the curtains, trying to see who was there.

"There's a big crowd," he whispered. "All your brothers and sisters, Roberto. And look! Leroy and his gang. And in the corner, those kids who were fishing. And, oh, no! Here come the birdwatchers. This is terrible, they're going to hate us. We might as well go home now."

Just then the curtains were swept back...

"Come on," said Tex, "we can only do our best," and they went straight into "The Grizzly Bear Stomp".

"I'm a grizzly bear," sang Bruno,
"I've got frizzly hair
I want to rock and roll,
Like an electric mole."

But while he was singing Bruno could hear shouts coming from the audience:

"TURN IT UP!"
"LOUDER!"
"WE CAN'T HEAR!"
"NOT LOUD ENOUGH!"

"Did you hear that, boys?" said Bruno, when they'd finished the song. "They want us to play louder. OK," said Bruno, turning everything on full, "let 'em have it."

The noise was deafening!

But the audience loved it.

The noise was terrific!

But that's how they wanted it.

The Donuts finished their second song.

"Funny, isn't it?" said Bruno. "Yesterday we were too loud for this crowd, today we can't be loud enough. Sometimes you just can't win! Come on, kids, let's give it to 'em again!"

And the band played on.

Text and illustrations Copyright ©1983 by Colin McNaughton
All rights reserved, including the right to reproduce this
book or portions thereof in any form.
Published in the United States by
Holt, Rinehart and Winston, 383 Madison Avenue,
New York, New York 10017.

Originally published in Great Britain by William Heinemann Ltd.

Library of Congress Cataloging in Publication Data

McNaughton, Colin.
Crazy bear.

Contents: Cowboy crazy—Snow crazy—Pirate crazy
—Rock and roll crazy.
1. Children's stories, English. [1. Bears—Fiction.
2. Animals—Fiction. 3. Short stories] I. Title.
PZ7.M23256Cr 1983   [E]   82-23372
ISBN 0-03-063043-6

First American Edition
Printed in Singapore
1 3 5 7 9 10 8 6 4 2